AF347917

Murmurs Of A Poet

On Love, Nature & Spirituality.

ISBN: 978-93-6123-979-3
Published by: Shiva Scribes

Shiva Scribes

shivascribes@gmail.com

First Edition: December 2023

For permissions, contact:
shivascribes@gmail.com

This book is dedicated to my Incorporeal teacher and

life coach Father Shiva.

Contents

Introduction

Poetry has been one of the prominent modes of artistic expression throughout history. It is like a delicate dance between language and emotion, transcending the constraints of prose and offering a canvas where feelings and thoughts unfold with musical grace. Poetry holds a significant amount of freedom and musicality, which has, for centuries, kept the interest in this art form alive. The emotions that poems carry and the messages they convey can be profoundly deep, yet they achieve this with utmost economy, using the fewest words possible.

The beauty of poetry lies not just in the words used but also in the spaces between the words and the unspoken nuances, allowing the reader to bring their interpretations and visualizations to life. It is an art form that transcends the boundaries of time, as the emotions captured in the verses remain timeless.

"Murmurs of A Poet" is a miscellaneous collection of such insightful poems on various aspects of life. These poems illuminate the path to inner awakening, ignite the curiosity to look within and explore love, truth, freedom, and the profound connection we share with nature.

Wings of Liberation

Freedom is our birthright; hence bondage doesn't feel

light.

In captivity, a soul cries, when can't use its wings to

fly.

How innocent are we, we act unwittingly,

We create our cage and then weep inside profusely.

This cage is of the mind, not of any metal,

let go of all resistance, it is all mental.

Release at this moment, what is holding you down,

How can we move with this baggage all around?

This life is beautiful, but only if we can,

spread our wings and fly, my friend

This life is a gift to sing and dance.

The New Man

Climbing the ladder up a step, or two, then

descending again,

A butterfly still in the cocoon, trying to break free

from the chains.

On the tight-rope held between the two mountains

I walk,

An arduous, nevertheless, incredible

unending mission

I should undertake, for me to cross.

With no other recourse for redemption

from these chains

I muster up my courage and commence. I sleep, I

slip, I slumber.

Standing up again, gathering scattered pieces of my

faith together,

I shake off the doubts and start again.

With danger lurking on both sides; one future,
one side past
A thin tightrope to tread upon — this moment,
as it lasts.
Getting swayed by either side or being pulled
by the flesh,
A moment of distraction, Snap! I've got to
start afresh.

This is just not my expedition, at some point,
of every man
To find that which is unchanging — stillness, inside
With absolute bliss and deep silence unwavering,
At peace with what is; knowing both pleasure and
pain are fleeting.

A state where our hearts be filled with grace
As royal swans, we'll gently breeze through the lake.
That day isn't far, where men will be sublime.
Its coming will mark the birth of — The New Man

The Unflickering Flame

You are a bright lamp

in this absolute darkness.

A guiding light

for this hurtling world.

How can your light

be flickering?

You are not a star

far away that you flicker.

You are a star on earth.

Shine bright.

Allow your radiance

to shine through the veil of night.

You are here for others,

Preserve your light.

One Step of Courage

Today is the day, do what matters to you

What is stopping you, friend,

To live a life of truth.

It is long overdue, it is now or never,

Bid the doubts adieu.

The judgments you hold,

the narrowing beliefs you carry,

are nothing but just a point of view.

Let go of what obstructs the new,

sit, perform a genuine review.

Listen to what your heart says,

You can hear it in your silent rendezvous.

Every step you take unafraid,

The universe will reciprocate

Guiding you to a breakthrough…

Sight Scenes

On our way, as we move ahead
things unfurl, pulling our attention.
Sometimes salty, at times sweet
occasionally bitter, not to mention.

We crave what feels good
avert which feels bitter,
regardless, we get entangled
in either one or the other.

Knowing what all happens,
is for us to learn
to propel us forward,
towards what we truly yearn.
Allow things to be, don't entwine,
Simply be an observer,
keep on marching,

this is your time.

These are only sight scenes
wasting time would be treason,
to your inner sovereignty,
realize this now, in a second.

Learn what you ought to, move on,
Keep your eye on your destination.
Remind yourself of the fact
all happens for a reason.

Our Bodies Many Cries

Every time the body aches in tension

or settles to create pain,

It is trying to bring your attention

to itself, by resorting to complaints.

Just as a child cries at times

when it wants to get parents' heed

The body pleads in pain to say,

"Please change your deeds!".

"I served you since your birth", it says,

"Please don't disregard,

I have allowed you to express and served you well,

Please give me your love, it ain't that hard"

It is such a gift this body of ours

Which allows us to play-

To see, to listen, to dance and sing

How much one should love, I say.

The Crow

Sitting on a bench in this nature's nook in noon
Amidst the plants cleansed after the monsoon.
The grass had outgrown its usual size;
Perhaps the gardener is waiting
to trim after the monsoon reign subsides.

As I was basking in the moist fresh air
I sensed a lively creature's playful cheer.
Upon a barrow parked close and clear
An innocent crow hopped around,
Looking around swiftly, there and here.

I wondered, how come I always judged
this being to be ugly and cacophonous?
It is simply being how it is designed to be
It is the creator who takes the onus.

Accept the regret I express for the biased sight
This prejudiced lens colored the inner light
I acknowledge you are innocent and bright
How could I not see? musing…in hindsight.

Celebrating Beauty

In the fiery pull of desires flame,
We wander around in winding bylanes,
Seeking expansion beyond measure
But getting lost time and again.

You have the whole world to revel,
The majestic mountains stand serene,
Deepest oceans whisper untold tales,
Purest rivers and lakes flow pristine.

Then why confine yourself to alleys,
When the world awaits your presence?
These desires lead you nowhere
When you already are full in your essence.

Quiet your inner tumult, be still,
Celebrate the beauty that surrounds.

For in embracing the world with open will,

You'll find tranquility, where no desire is found.

Beings Of Light

They ask—"Why are you so aloof?

Whatever happens, you don't mind"

I say, "I don't belong to this world

rather someplace else,

Look inside, that is what you too will find"

"If we don't belong here, as you say

then why are we here", they ask,

"We've come to express

and for play, not for any task"

This story is not just ours I say

But for every being in sight,

We may be dwelling in this world

But we belong to the world of light.

I Remember You

I wake up at the crack of dawn,
before the horizon
of night and day.
The stars are glimmering yet
about to fade away.

I embrace this new day
bidding yesterday adieu,
With love and gratitude
I remember you.

I go for a stroll
I see the open sky,
So clear and pristine,
and birds flying high.

The dancing of the trees

Murmurs of A Poet

to the tune of the breeze,
that rustling sound
with those little squirrels
running around.

The sound of the waves
hitting the shore,
blended with the music
of the breeze and the birds.

I take a deep breath,
Rejoicing, in the sheer beauty
Of Mother Earth.
With Gratitude,
I remember you.

I take a pause,
I look within
I remember me,
I remember you

Adulterated

I came into this world
so pristine,
looking at it
in all its newness.

Filled with wonder
as I saw things around,
The beauty each color exuded
it put me in awe.

I looked into the eyes
of the woman I was held by,
Looking at me
With intense love and joy.

In absolute surrender,
trusting in her galore,

Murmurs of A Poet

I am taken care of
I'll be provided for.

With no trace of self
just truly living,
On my cradle
Rejoicing and swinging.

Then the inevitable happened,
something I didn't see coming;
before I knew it,
I was Adult-erated.

The Tree

The seed patiently waits
pushing through the soil with gentle force,
To bring forth a delicate sapling to the world
In absolutely no hurry to grow.

Making most of what life offers;
Growing with the love of the sun,
along with air, mud, and water
Years later this glorious tree stands tall

Bending down to share its fruits,
Pretty flowers, and fresh air to breathe,
Much needed shade to the traveler
The humble tree just gives.

In autumn, it lets go of its leaves
It does so without crying or clinging.

Murmurs of A Poet

In summer, its crown is dense
It shares with the world without thinking.

Seasons come, seasons go.
Not holding on to what has done
Swaying along with the gentle breeze
This content tree is at ease.

Existence is so beautiful
Inspiring in every way
Feel the one which is breathing
It is only that which is worth being anyway.

I Want To Be A Book

I don't wish to share
With anyone, anything,
which is not flowing
in my veins yet.

I don't wish to preach-
What is right or wrong,
Who am I to decide?
What difference does it make?

I don't wish to counsel
For maybe it's an assumed insight,
When I think 'I know',
the truth takes flight.

The very thought,
reveals how much I don't,

This thought will keep
the 'I am' forever obscured.

I don't want to speak a thing
I don't want to dwell in knowing,
I want to swim,
In the vast ocean of being.

Silent like a book
my story unfolds,
In these quiet words,
It says it all.

Fills Me With Hope

In the midst of such drudgery
In all this disorder and deceit
Seeing a fellow man helping another
Fills me with hope and wonder.

Humans exploiting their own mother
Using and abusing to no end
But when I see some other
Plant a tree, caring for her,
I am filled with hope and wonder.

With all the noise out there, and in;
I go in that space of silence within,
That spark of love, the prevalent order,
Covertly hiding under all disorder
Fills me with immense hope
and a sense of wonder.

Stars of The Earth

The sun hasn't quite set yet
But the moon is already out,
Couldn't wait to share its beauty
With everyone around.

The Sky is waiting now
To be decorated with stars,
Their twinkling lights
Amplifying this breathtaking -
Show of the Universe

This universe is playful,
Birds singing, sun shining,
Dolphins playfully swimming across
Trees dancing to the tune of the wind.

When we are one with it

With all of creation
We become shining stars
Frolicking on the earth

Such stars radiate light,
guiding others.
Making them a part of
This unique galaxy of stars
Who trod upon this earth.

Natures Art

I sit and look at the ocean for hours
Listening the sound of its waves
Gently hitting the shore
Reflecting the rays of the sun
Which covertly comes through
From the gaps between the clouds.

The sun is calling a wrap to this day
Leaving behind varied colors in the sky
The birds flying back to their nests
Or wherever they stay
Bidding everyone goodbye.

To sit back and joyfully witness
The Majestic entry of the moon
With its entourage of stars
This inexplicable and ineffable splendor

Of Mother Earth, touches the heart,

There is this feeling engendered--

How wonderful is Nature's Art.

The Kiss

I took a stroll on a serene evening
Along the seaside in an otherwise buzzing city.
With cool breeze, gently caressing,
Under the vast sky so pretty
Having kids and pets playing,
jumping around merrily.

In the midst of all this bustling,
I saw two lovers passionately kissing.
When a wave of love rises between two,
So much that words don't come to avail,
Two sets of lips come together
Expressing where words failed.

Right behind them in the distant horizon
Under the colorful sky
The sun gently kissed the sea

Only to disappear away in a while,

Leaving behind as a gift to all

the radiant sensuous sky.

The Great Mother

I remember as a child,
Coming home after being ridiculed
At times chided by the teacher
When I was downhearted
I took refuge in the lap of my mother.

I remember being heart-broken
Spending hours by the sea shore
In the company of the sky and ocean,
To mend my broken heart
Nature's embrace was my cushion.

Now that I long to break free
From this noise
Of desires and expectations
To maintain an everlasting poise
I take refuge in my spiritual heart.

When the dim and noise become

Overwhelmingly turbulent,

I let go and surrender

I take refuge in God,

The Great Mother.

That Secret Ingredient

One does something, anything,

Some judge it to be 'good'

Others deduce it to be 'bad'

But they miss out on what is unseen.

That secret ingredient-

The intent, it is that which comes back.

Something happens or the other

We sulk and at times wonder

Lamenting over - Why me? Why not others?

We miss out on what is unseen

That secret ingredient-

It is what we have sent out, coming hither.

Mother cooks for her child

A lover for its beloved

Their bond is thus strengthened

It's not the taste or condiment
It is that secret ingredient-
Love, which makes it a delicacy.

Becoming

I was gazing outside my window
Watching birds doing their dance,
Each singing their tune which somehow
Miraculously came together as a perfect song!
As I was enjoying this little yet profound
show of mother nature, I saw a little lower
a gentle and lovely black and red butterfly.
frolicking upon the flowers.
This light-footed nimble creature,
gentle and at the same time lively
Leaping from one flower to another
Dancing in all its glory.
A caterpillar may have once hung
Upside down swaddling itself,
in silk, with great struggle
Came out as this royal butterfly.

Life at times too is overwhelming,

Enveloping us in its tight cocoon.

It does so for us to metamorphosize

For just like the butterfly,

This cocoon is for our 'Becoming'.

Language

I am sitting here with my pen
and a book in hand,
waiting for words to appear in my mind.
An attempt to cook something up
perhaps a bit nice and kind.

These words at times I feel,
have their own constraints.
How can I write about that
Which can only be felt?

I have got no words, staring at the page
then at the wall,
Looking at the lizard skid away
searching for a fly,
in vain, just as I.

Reminds me of the wall
we built inside our hearts,
Obstructing the cool breeze of love to pass
Making our hearts to wither,
devoid of the nectar of love.

Break this wall of language
End this drought of love.
You and I ain't different,
We are one

Soul Bird

Hey Soul Bird!

You have been in this jail from eons,

Having forgotten you are a free bird.

Ego has cut your wings and has you entrapped,

You don't belong here

Then why don't you fly away.

Hey Soul Bird, Fly!

Don't be in this prison anymore

You are meant to fly

Be what you are meant to be

A bird flying in the sky.

Hey Soul Bird Fly!

Escape from this prison

Using the wings of Silence

Don't get pulled back.

What is in the jail?

Other than slavery and lack.

Hey Soul Bird, Fly!
You were born to dwell high.
Spread the wings of Silence and Fly!
Don't get trapped in what you see
When you have experienced the beauty
and the magnificence of the unseen.
Spread those wings wide,
Soul Bird, Fly!

In the Cottage of my Forehead

In the midst of upheaval
Of corrupt minds creating ruckus
Egos coming together
Seeing each other as separate.
In this endeavor for instant pleasure,
We invite pain into our lives
It is time to go back to the cottage
It is there we will feel truly alive.

In the midst of all this competition,
We disregard cooperation
In this futile thirst for power
Ourselves destroying our own generation.
In this venture to grab power
We invite powerlessness into our lives
It is time to go back in the cottage
It is only there we will feel truly alive.

The conflicts outside,

a reflection of the ones within.

It is for each of us to observe

Allow the dust to settle through

It is only when we bring our attention

Into the cottage in our forehead

We can see his reflection.

The Dark Night of the Soul

In this dark night of the soul,

When the glimmer of hope

is flickering into obscurity.

Humanity creating illusionary walls

within, unwelcoming, with insecurity.

Where beings are not respected

loved and cared for,

How easily and indifferently,

snatching away one's right to be.

Callously hurting one another.

When the river of love

seems to have dried and receded

And compassion seems

to be in oblivion in the face of pride.

Humanity is trapped in a cage

of their own making

screaming and crying inside.

It is this dark night of the soul,

where one becomes tired of sickness,

One turns inward, opens their heart.

Allowing the light to seep in,

breaking the shackles apart.

This light brings forth compassion,

and the river springs to life again.

This dark night of the soul

is the darkness, just before,

the beginning of a new dawn.

Mend A Broken Heart

Most of us are bestowed at birth
The gift of a broken heart.
Such a one will try his best
Not to break another's
For having been through the pain
He wishes not to inflict the same on others.

A broken heart is a gem
It is in this ruin one finds a treasure.
Like fire purifies gold
the pain refines them.
In anguish, towards God he moves,
His love transforms and hurls.

Accepting the fragments,
embracing it with openness
Gently being with it

accepting the darkness.
Allows the heart to rest,
healing the scars,
Revealing to us the secrets of the stars.

A broken heart is a blessing.
It is a doorway to truth;
A push from divine grace
to drop the veil of illusion.
You have been now for too along apart
Love is the only way
to mend a broken heart.

Thy Will Be Done

My heart is in fragments
One piece is running in one direction
one in another.
A silent skirmish within
A battleground for tug and pulls.

I am travelling with this baggage;
eyes weary, legs debilitated,
All energy seems drained,
Tired of fulfilling the whims.
I want to let go all will of mine,
and surrender to your will, divine.

I have no will of my own
Your will is mine.
In my heart, I want
you to be the only one.

Not my, but let thy will be done.

The Ocean Spoke to Me

Besides her, I took my seat
To be graced in her company.
Her gentle music filled the air,
A harmony that chased away despair.

A message sought release
In this quiet space,
Listening to her whispering song,
Her alluring voice, beckoned me along.

The waves conversed in rhythmic tone,
"Feel it now, as you sit alone.
Deep as the ocean, your essence lies,
A treasure vast beneath, which never dies."

"Do you harness the depths within?
Where immense wisdom and wonders begin"

The Ocean implores, in its silent plea,
Observe closely, let your spirit be free.

So, I sat in silence, heeding the call,
To unravel the mysteries and clear my vision,
The Ocean is trying to tell me something
Only if I am ready to listen.

Her Naked Beauty in the Moonlight

He saw her naked in the moonlight,
and stood in awe,
drifted into an ineffable sight.
He saw her sparkling eyes,
their silent depth unfolding.
He saw her naked beauty
in the moonlight.

She opened herself,
revealing her true self.
Her honesty touched his heart—
it takes courage to lower our guard,
to reveal the heart as it is,
to embrace all that we are,
both light and dark.

Murmurs of A Poet

He saw her naked beauty
in the moonlight.

She cast away her masks,
stripped of all that was borrowed,
and stood in her truth—
powerful, yet gentle in humility.

She became a mirror
to all who looked upon her.
He saw his own shadows,
and glimpsed his hidden light.

For the first time,
he found himself naked
in that moonlit night.

Breeze

I can hear you

I can feel you

Gently making the trees rustle

You caress me,

Play with the strands of my hair,

You give me a cool and calm

feel, making sure,

you are here, I'm aware.

Just as you carry with you

grains of sand as you blow,

Take the layers off me

flow through me,

Take with you everything

Which is untrue

So I am only left with the truth.

Madness

It is madness to hate all roses
coz once you were hurt by a thorn.

It is madness to give up on your dreams
coz your failed attempts made you worn.

It is madness to stop trusting
coz once your trust has been torn.

It is madness to keep looking for joy
Even though you still haven't found.

In this madness, we lose ourselves,
You like being mad?
Then be mad in love.

Lighthouse

Walk the path of light
Walk the path of truth
Even if it is only you alone,
Don't follow the world
For they do know not where they roam,
Follow your heart
For it knows its way back home.
Be silent, listen to what is inside,
You may stumble, but be strong,
Worry not for morrow, have faith
You have been taken care of all along.
Walk the path of light
Walk the path of truth
Don't entertain fear,
For only those, my dear
who walk the path of light
Become a lighthouse for all here.

From the Shores of the Ocean

You have now come drifting

to the shores of the ocean

through his grace,

without your intention.

Here you are at this junction

You ought to make a decision

Will you go back?

Or will you plunge in the ocean?

There is a tussle

of tug and pull,

between your heart

and what you think is you.

Who will win?

Which one will you feed?

Murmurs of A Poet

Which one will you pay heed to?
Which one would you cheer for?

You have to take a call.
The boat of truth won't sail
If it doesn't leave the shore
Living short of its destiny.

Womb of Purity

I look inside, I see movements
I see light, I see some darkness
Which doesn't belong,
Obscuring the beautiful light of dawn.

With the fire of love,
I clean those bits of dirt
To create space for my beloved
With whom I wish to flirt.

As I dwell in myself
I dwell in you
In this womb of purity
I feel no blues

It is here when I
feel the lord

Sucking the nectar

from the breast of god.

Nothing Ever Stays

I see everything move
Pain comes and leaves
Pleasure comes and disappears too
Nothing here ever holds true
Nothing ever stays but you.

Thoughts come like puffs of cloud
fill the sky all around
Soon the sun shines through
Leaving the sky wide with bright hue,
Nothing ever stays but you.

I see everything move,
Sensations come and leave,
Emotions come and disappears too,
Nothing here ever holds true,
Nothing ever stays but you.

Nothing we experience is true,
Our perception makes things so,
Everything we hold on to,
We try hard but it still slips through,
Nothing ever stays but you.

The Gift of Present

Moments are passing by,
As I write under this moonlit night
Each moment comes
As a present for me to live it right.
The moon is in its full luminescence
Clouds are gently floating in the sky
I stand as a witness
Allowing them to pass by
Basking in the magnificence of the Moon.
The beauty of the moon,
its gleam, is missed,
when I flow with the clouds.
Why follow the clouds,
When I can bathe in the glory of the moon?

Reconsider

What is it that you yearn for?

Will it truly quench your thirst?

Why the need for expectations?

What is it you want from people?

Why this ceaseless seeking, stumbling door to door?

Having found nothing on the other side,

Wallowing in the futility of the pursuit,

a relentless search, have you ever found it?

In the quiet chambers of introspection,

Find the essence of contentment.

Maybe it's time to turn within,

Maybe, it's time to reconsider.

The Boatman

Under the ever-shifting sky,

My boat dances on tides high and low

When high, my boat shakes and quivers,

I find faith slipping away from my fingers

Doubts and fears stealthy creeps in

What if the water gets within?

Yet, you arrive, a gentle presence,

Whispering truths of impermanence.

"Let the tides pass, don't cling," you say,

In front of this boat of truth,

these tides won't last.

The boatman is not just any,

It is the powerhouse.

Guiding through tides, a force to espouse.

I find my heart flushed with faith abound.

I am sitting on this boat of truth

sailing around.

The Dog

A dog lying down on an empty street
Bewildered, seeing the humans vanish suddenly.
An occasional chirping of the bird
here - then there - fills the silence
which prevails, devoid of the noise of the herd.

The herd, spending most of the day
Inside what they call the prison
of four walls, binging on TV,
having nothing to do
Filling self with all that negativity.

Seeing everyone play the game
With no one taking the onus
We all seem so riven
Time has come to teach us
But we ain't learning the lesson

This happened to humble us
To bring us out of the bubble
this dream of the ego
To reveal, arrogance and our love for power
Doesn't work, but we ain't letting it go.

Meanwhile, the dog oblivious to everything
Takes a nap in its unobtrusive world
Being here without the worry of the morrow
When the herd is in the grasp of fear.

The Rosary

I remember, at twilight,

when I was a child,

my grandma sitting in the balcony,

chanting all the while.

With a rosary in her hand

and a silent intoxication in her eyes,

Remembering with deep love

the grace of divine.

The beads of rosary,

binded by the thread

Sticking to each other,

not repelling instead.

We all belong to one

we are in this together,

In this rosary of Humanity

it is love which is what binds us.

When this thread is broken,

the beads fall apart

scattering everywhere forgetting

it is the Rosary Of Humanity

of which we are a part.

The Tower of Peace

I observe my mind,

Allow it to settle down

I reach a space within,

Absolutely still.

In this quiet space,

I am peace,

In this silent chamber,

I am love

In this limitless depth,

I am joy

I won't allow anyone or anything

create ripples in the still lake of my mind.

I Am… the Tower of Peace.

Unperturbed, Unshakable

I Am…the Tower of Silence.

I Am…

Note from The Author

Dear Friend,

I thank you for spending your precious time
To read these words written from the heart,
I hope you found it worth,
and appreciate this little work of art.

I wanted to share my thoughts,
Express gratitude for your attention
This was the sole intention,
And of course, to cultivate my vibrations.

I wish you loads of joy and love,
I wish you success in all endeavors,
No matter who and where you are from,
I hope you find your inner treasure.

Murmurs of A Poet

If these words have moved you a bit,

Of something within you unspoken,

Then please share your love with others,

You never know whose heart is broken.

I pray we all step up to the vision-

The highest one we behold,

And may we have the courage,

the will, to let go of the old.

About the Author

Hi, I'm Varun Jain, a writer who has found writing to be a potent support on my transformative journey. My path as a writer is deeply intertwined with self-exploration, shaping my perspective on life and the human experience. Practicing Raja Yoga Meditation taught by the BrahmaKumaris World Spiritual University has been a significant part of this enriching journey.

I've discovered immense power in words, especially during moments of contemplation, where words have propelled me beyond words into a space of silence. Though I initially began my writing journey with prose, I occasionally felt that I was using too many words to express something that could be conveyed with fewer. The love for silence guided me to express myself with fewer words. The intention to convey my heart through the economical use of words is what

drove me toward poetry.

Website: https://www.varunx.com

84